To Noah,
Always remember,
you are so loved
no matter what!

1 John 4:19

I Would Love You Even If You Were A Pickle

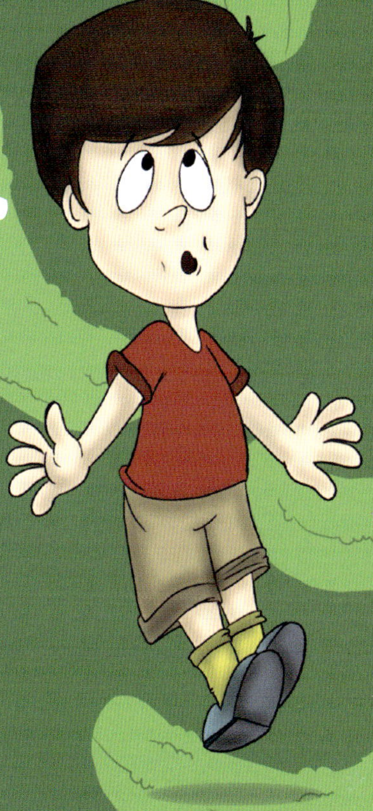

Bucleigh Newton Kernodle
illustrated by Ashley Teets

I Would Love You Even If You Were A Pickle

by Bucleigh Newton Kernodle
illustrated by Ashley Teets

To order additional copies of this book, or for book publishing information, or to contact the author:

Headline Kids
P. O. Box 52
Terra Alta, WV 26764

Email: mybook@headlinebooks.com
www.headlinebooks.com

Ashley Teets—*Art Director*
Lucas Kelly—*Design/Layout*

Published by Headline Books
Headline Kids is an imprint of Headline Books

ISBN-13: 9781946664525

Library of Congress Control Number: 2018960338

PRINTED IN THE UNITED STATES OF AMERICA

To my loving husband, my mother and my late father. I could not have written this without any of you. Thank you for all your insight, encouragement and motivation. You believed in me when I didn't believe in myself. Because of you, my dream is a reality.

To my son, Miller, your words inspire me. Our conversations bless me. You are my precious gift from above.

To my mentor and teacher Mike, I love writing because of you. I am grateful for your teachings and all your wisdom.

To all the children out there who need to be reminded that it's ok to make mistakes. It doesn't mean you are unloved.

And to our Heavenly Father who shows us unconditional love daily.

It was bedtime so his mommy tucked him in his bed, but Miller couldn't quite lay down his worried head.

"Mommy, I'm sorry I made a bad choice today. But will you still love me anyway?"

His mommy replied with what she knew to be true, "I will always love you no matter what you do."

"Thanks Mommy," he said, "but you know what? I would love you even if you were a pickle."

"Oh really? Well I would love you even if you were a leaky faucet that goes trickle, trickle, trickle!" said Mommy.

“Well, I would love you even if you were stinky cheese surrounded by buzzing bees,” said Miller.

“I would love you even if you were a tacky toad oozing slime by the boatload!” said Mommy.

"I would love you even if you were a cactus with too many spikes that strike. Yikes!" said Miller.

"I would love you even if you were a pesky pigeon not leaving anyone alone- not even a smidgen!" said Mommy.

"I would love you even if you were a greedy honey bear who doesn't share!" said Miller.

"I would love you even if you were a lazy hare playing foursquare in his underwear," said Mommy.

“I would love you even if you were a shrieking bat who sits on a doormat-beat that!” said Miller.

“Okay, I would love you even if you were spilled lemonade on a newly placed band-aid,” said Mommy.

“Wow! That sure is a lot of love!” Miller shouted.

“It is, Miller!” his mommy explained. “The love I have for you is like the love from above. God loves us no matter what. Whether we are small, big, tall, or stinky, He loves us from our heart to our pinky.”

He then laid down his head and she kissed him goodnight. Away he drifted off to sleep, as sweet dreams took flight.

ROAR!